Stress-Reducing Activities for Teens

Author: Alexis Fey
Contributor: Penni Ippensen, LCSW Therapist
Editor: Mary Dieterich
Proofreaders: Margaret Brown and Jennifer Hentzel

COPYRIGHT © 2024 Mark Twain Media, Inc.

ISBN 978-1-62223-894-1

Printing No. CD-405087

Mark Twain Media, Inc., Publishers
Distributed by Carson Dellosa Education

Table of Contents

Table of Contents (cont.)

Introduction

It is common for a young person to struggle with their mental health, which includes their mental, emotional, and social well-being. Everyone worries and feels anxious or sad from time to time, and children, unfortunately, are not immune to this. Studies have actually shown that Generation Z (people born between 1997 and 2012) are experiencing unprecedented amounts of anxiety and depression. This may sound daunting, but this activity book can help!

This book will provide a variety of activities and resources that are geared toward helping a young person cope with everyday stressors and mental health struggles. Each section will begin with an explanation of the topic for the parent or teacher and how the related activities can be used to help children cope. Following this explanation, there will be directions for the child or student on how to complete the activity, along with an example and space to complete it. The pages in this book are reproducible. Make the necessary copies for each child/student who will be completing the activities.

The child or student will be prompted to complete activities that not only help them cope with everyday worries, but also energize their brain and improve overall cognitive function. The activities can be completed in the order they are presented, or the user can flip through the book to complete activities that seem interesting to them. This book has activities that can be completed indoors as well as outdoors, making it a great resource regardless of the weather! It should also be noted that these activities are a far better alternative to unhealthy coping skills that children and teens often turn to such as drinking, smoking, driving fast in cars, being aggressive, avoiding loved ones, or pouring too much time into social media. Let's get working!

Coping Skills and Why They're Important

Life can feel really hard at times and that can leave a person, especially a child or teenager, feeling down and struggling with their mental health. It can be tempting to "tough it out" and wait for your circumstances to improve. It is important, though, to learn to cope and enjoy your  life while you are experiencing problems, because life will always have its problems. It can also be tempting to wait until you feel better to work on your mental health. But instead of waiting until you feel better to do something, you can do something to make yourself feel better! This is where coping skills come into play.

A **coping skill** is a thought or behavior that can help one calm down and manage a stressful situation that is being experienced. In a study completed in 2018, Edraki, Rambod, and Molazem found that "coping skills training reduced depression, anxiety and stress" in adolescents who were faced with severe psychological problems. Another study completed in 2017 showed that coping skills were essential to reducing behavior problems in adolescents (Modecki, Zimmer-Gembeck, & Guerra). When faced with anxiety or depression, there is no one magic solution.

There are different kinds of coping skills that are appropriate to use for different people and at different times, depending on the situation. The different categories of coping skills and examples of each are listed below.

- **Rest and relaxation** – an activity that calms you mentally and physically, such as taking a nap or foam rolling sore muscles after exercising

- **Companionship** – an activity that connects you with others, such as talking with a friend about a struggle you are currently experiencing

- **Health** – an activity that benefits your physical health, like eating a healthy meal or exercising

- **Distraction** – an activity, such as reading a good book, that distracts from what is currently stressing you out

- **Opposite action** – an activity that leaves you feeling positive and is the opposite of your impulse; examples of this include watching a funny movie or listening to a motivational speech

Coping Skills and Why They're Important (cont.)

- **Emotional awareness** – an activity that encourages you to identify and express your feelings, like journaling or drawing

- **Mindfulness** – an activity that brings your mind to the present moment only, like meditation or belly breathing exercises

- **Spirituality** – an activity that connects you to your inner spirit and/or the spirit of a higher power, such as prayer or spending intentional time in nature

In this activity book, you will have the opportunity to practice all the coping skill categories listed above in some capacity. This will allow you to practice and learn which coping skills work best for you. It is important to practice coping skills when you feel good and are not stressed so that when it comes time to use them, you already know how and which ones work for you. And finally, there is no one magic solution for depression and anxiety. Because of this, a combination approach using a variety of coping skills, and possibly therapy and psychotropic medication, will yield the best results.

Releasing Your Tension Through Writing

Teacher/Parent Introduction

This section empowers the student to process and overcome their mental health struggles, whether that be anxiety, depression, ADHD, or even just enduring a hard day, through writing. The first activity, *Building Yourself Up*, encourages the student to remember what makes them unique and valued. In middle-school, children are beginning to become aware of themselves and how they relate to others. While this is a normal stage of a child's development, the constant comparing of themselves to others can lead to low self-esteem. By answering the prompts in the following activity, the child will remember all the things that make them special. This activity is an example of an opposite action coping skill, as it helps the student contradict the negative emotions they may be feeling.

The next activity, *Learning to See the Positives*, is all about practicing gratitude. Practicing gratitude means to acknowledge something you are thankful for, and it is one of the easiest ways to improve a person's mood. It will help your teen deal with adversity and has been clinically proven to decrease depression and anxiety. You get more of what you look for, so the more your teen tries to find something to be thankful for, the more they will be thankful for! To reap maximum benefits, this is something that should be incorporated into the student's daily routine.

This activity is an example of a few different kinds of coping skills. The gratitude activity exemplifies a distraction coping skill in that it helps take your mind off the stressful situation at hand. It exemplifies opposite action in that it leaves you feeling positive despite enduring a situation that had you feeling negatively before. And it exemplifies mindfulness in that it helps you focus on the present moment.

The final activity, *Mindfulness Journaling for Mental Health,* will provide the student with many open-ended journal prompts to help them process their emotions. A journal is a safe place to explore thoughts and feelings without the judgment of others. Journaling will teach the student how to slow down, observe their world, and reflect on what is important to them. Did they have a stressful day with a lot of emotions? Writing out what happened can help them make sense of everything. Did they have a really great day with a lot of laughter? They should describe in detail what happened that made that day fun so they never forget it. Journaling helps a person practice emotional awareness and mindfulness, as it forces them to think through and identify the emotions that they are currently feeling. Writing in a journal is the perfect outlet for thoughts and feelings of any kind and is a great life-long habit to begin forming.

Name: Date:

Student Activities: Building Yourself Up

Instructions: Answer the following prompts as a way to build your self-esteem and focus on the positives to help you overcome mental health struggles or even just a bad day.

I am good at…

1. _______________________________

2. _______________________________

3. _______________________________

I've helped others by…

1. _______________________________

2. _______________________________

3. _______________________________

Compliments I have received…

1. _______________________________

2. _______________________________

3. _______________________________

Things that make me unique…

1. _______________________________

2. _______________________________

3. _______________________________

What I like about my appearance…

1 _______________________________

2. _______________________________

3. _______________________________

What I value the most…

1. _______________________________

2. _______________________________

3. _______________________________

Challenges I have overcome…

1. _______________________________

2. _______________________________

3. _______________________________

Times I've made others happy…

1. _______________________________

2. _______________________________

3. _______________________________

Student Activities: Learning to See the Positives

Instructions: On your own sheet of paper, answer the following prompts in detail. If you enjoy this activity and want to continue practicing gratitude even after you have completed all the following prompts, you can simply take a few minutes each day and write down something you are grateful for, no matter how big or small.

1. What made you smile today?

2. Who are you grateful for, and what do you love about them?

3. What do you like about the current season?

4. What is something that was hard to do but you did it anyway?

5. What is something you love in nature?

6. Who makes you feel loved and how?

7. Name someone who was nice to you and what they did that was nice.

8. Who is your best friend and why?

9. What do you like most about your school?

10. What is the best gift you have ever received?

11. What is your favorite hobby and why?

12. Where is your favorite place to play or relax?

13. What is your favorite game or sport and why?

14. What is your favorite tv show or movie and why?

15. What is your favorite smell and why?

16. List three things you are excited for.

17. What is something that makes you laugh every time you hear or think about it?

18. What is an accomplishment you are proud of?

19. What is something in the room with you right now that you are thankful for?

20. Name a song that makes you feel happy.

Student Activities: Mindfulness Journaling for Mental Health

Instructions: Answer the following prompts with as much detail as you can muster on your own sheet of paper or in your own notebook.

1. How do you feel right now, in this moment? Intentionally pause and notice any sensations that you are feeling—your breath, the range of your emotions, something that's worrying you right now. Write it all down.

2. Describe the perfect way to spend the weekend. Who do you want to spend it with, if anyone, and what do you want to do? Write it all down in great detail.

3. Describe a difficult situation that you experienced and how you overcame it. If you are still in the middle of the difficult situation, brainstorm possible solutions.

4. If you were trapped on a deserted island and could only bring three recreational items, what would they be and why?

5. What does your dream house look like? Explain in detail the kinds of rooms you want to have, how many and what you want them to look like. What do you want the outside of your house to look like? Where do you want it to be located? Who do you envision yourself living with, if anyone?

6. Explain a time when you had a bad attitude about something. What happened, who was there, and what caused you to have a negative outlook on the situation? If you had to experience the same situation again, what could you do to have a better attitude?

7. Write about the strangest dream you have ever had. Explain every detail you can remember. Who was there? What did you see? What did you hear? What did you say? What was happening? How were you feeling?

8. Explain one thing that makes you anxious that you wish you could stop worrying about. Is there anything you can do to lessen this worry? If not, how can you healthily cope with the situation moving forward?

9. What personality traits do you appreciate most about yourself? What are some personality traits that you wish you could change? If desired, how could you go about changing those personality traits?

10. What three things do you want other people (family, friends, teachers, mentors, etc.) to know about you?

Student Activities: Mindfulness Journaling for Mental Health (cont.)

If you enjoy journaling and feel the benefits of expressing yourself through writing, here are some shorter everyday prompts that you could complete in a notebook of your own as part of your daily routine.

- What is something that made you laugh today?
- What steps did you take today toward a goal you're working on?
- Who made your day better today? How can you pay that feeling forward?
- What is one thing you want to remember from today?
- When did you feel most authentically yourself today?
- How can you make tomorrow (even) better than today?
- If you could be any animal, what would it be and why?
- What do you want to do with your life when you grow up and why?
- What would you do if you won the lottery?
- What is the most difficult part of everyday life?
- If you found a magical portal that could take you anywhere instantly, where would you go and why?
- What are some recent inventions that you think are dangerous to society?
- If you could have a dinner party and invite anyone in the world, who would you invite and why?
- If you could travel anywhere in the world for any amount of time regardless of how much it cost, where would you go and how long would you stay? Would you take anyone with you?
- What is your favorite subject in school and why?
- If you could use a time machine to travel to any time period in history, which time period would you choose and why?
- If you could meet any famous person, living or dead, who would it be and why? What would you say to them?

Feeling Crafty to Stop the Stress

Teacher/Parent Introduction

This section will allow the student to tap into their creative side with coloring pages, doodle prompts and multiple craft activities. Coloring can be cathartic, relaxing, and a fun way to get the mind off life's struggles. In addition to experiencing the pride of creating something beautiful, coloring has also been proven to relieve stress, calm an over-stimulated brain, and relax a tense body. Coloring is also a good tool to practice mindfulness, which is when the brain is tuned to focus only on the present, by carefully choosing colors and focusing enough to stay in the lines as the coloring pages are completed.

Like coloring, drawing can also be a relaxing method to distract the mind from current struggles while also energizing the brain and helping one practice mindfulness. Drawing allows one to get creative and express their feelings, which is what makes it a great example of an emotional awareness coping skill. Prompts are provided for the student to help get them started, but they can also draw something on their own sheet of paper.

Finally, art and craft activities are not only good distraction techniques to cope with mental health struggles, but they also provide an opportunity to become aware of and express any emotions that need to be processed. Art has been shown to reduce feelings of depression and anxiety by relaxing a person, relieving stress, and providing distance from negative thoughts and feelings.

If your teen enjoys completing art activities and is currently struggling with a mental disorder such as anxiety, depression, ADHD, etc., they might be a good candidate for art therapy. In short, art therapy is facilitated by a professional art therapist and, through art-making and creativity, helps a child build self-esteem, self-awareness, and emotional resistance and overcome feelings of anxiety and depression. For more information on art therapy, visit <www.arttherapy.org>.

Name: Date:

Student Activities: Coloring the Stress Away

Instructions: Using crayons, colored pencils, or gel pens, complete the coloring page with a lot of color. Choose colors that reflect how you are feeling or what you are going through. As you color, focus on your breathing—make sure that you are intentionally taking deep and steady breaths.

Name: Date:

Student Activities: Coloring the Stress Away (cont.)

Instructions: Using crayons, colored pencils, or gel pens, complete the coloring page with a lot of color. Choose colors that reflect how you are feeling or what you are going through. As you color, focus on your breathing—make sure that you are intentionally taking deep and steady breaths.

Name: Date:

Student Activities: Coloring the Stress Away (cont.)

Instructions: Using crayons, colored pencils, or gel pens, complete the coloring page with a lot of color. Choose colors that reflect how you are feeling or what you are going through. As you color, focus on your breathing—make sure that you are intentionally taking deep and steady breaths.

Name: Date:

Student Activities: Coloring the Stress Away (cont.)

Instructions: Using crayons, colored pencils, or gel pens, complete the coloring page with a lot of color. Choose colors that reflect how you are feeling or what you are going through. As you color, focus on your breathing—make sure that you are intentionally taking deep and steady breaths.

Name: Date:

Student Activities: Coloring the Stress Away (cont.)

Instructions: Using crayons, colored pencils, or gel pens, complete the coloring page with a lot of color. Choose colors that reflect how you are feeling or what you are going through. As you color, focus on your breathing—make sure that you are intentionally taking deep and steady breaths.

Name: Date:

Student Activities: Coloring the Stress Away (cont.)

Instructions: Using crayons, colored pencils, or gel pens, complete the coloring page with a lot of color. Choose colors that reflect how you are feeling or what you are going through. As you color, focus on your breathing—make sure that you are intentionally taking deep and steady breaths.

Name: Date:

Student Activities: Stop Worrying, Start Doodling!

1. In the box below, use crayons, colored pencils, or gel pens to draw a rainbow. Add scenery around the rainbow—maybe a blue sky in the background with a grassy meadow full of trees and wildflowers. Use your imagination!

2. In the box below, draw your favorite animal. This drawing can be as simple or as detailed as you prefer. If you are not sure how to get started, use the internet to research a simple drawing of the desired animal. Don't forget to add a lot of color to make the drawing look more realistic.

Name: Date:

Student Activities: Stop Worrying, Start Doodling! (cont.)

3. In the box below, draw a waterfall. This waterfall could be over the side of a mountain, in a jungle, or somewhere imaginary and unrealistic! Use your imagination and lots of color to make this scene come to life.

4. In the box below, draw a sunset. This sunset could be over a body of water, rolling hills, flat plains, through mountains, or anywhere else you can imagine. Use lots of vibrant colors and be sure to add details that make this sunset look realistic.

Name: Date:

Student Activities: Stop Worrying, Start Doodling! (cont.)

5. In the box below, draw a beach. Be sure to include common elements like the body of water, sand, sky, and maybe some people enjoying recreational time together. As always, use lots of color and detail in your drawing.

6. In the box below, draw a scene with your favorite flowers, trees, or other plants. If you need to, search online for pictures of what the leaves, blooms, bark, or other parts of the plants look like. You can be as realistic as you want or just draw an impression of the plants. Use lots of vibrant colors and add details to make your plants look alive.

Student Activities: DIY Activities

DIY Bath Bomb

Materials:

½ cup baking soda

¼ cup citric acid (You can purchase this at most specialty food or ethnic grocery stores or online.)

¼ cup cornstarch

¼ cup Epsom salt

3 teaspoons castor oil (or any vegetable oil)

1 teaspoon of any essential oil to achieve the desired scent

Soap coloring or food coloring

1 tablespoon water (This amount can vary slightly depending on the humidity level where you live.)

Soap mold or plastic ornament mold (can be found at most craft stores)

Instructions:

1. Mix the dry ingredients in a large bowl – ½ cup baking soda, ¼ cup citric acid, ¼ cup cornstarch, and ¼ cup Epsom salt.

2. In a cup or small bowl, combine the wet ingredients – 3 teaspoons castor oil, 1 teaspoon of essential oil, soap or food coloring as desired, 1 tablespoon water.

3. Add the liquid mixture to the dry mixture a very small amount at a time and begin whisking to combine.

4. When both mixtures are well combined into one, tightly pack the mixture into the mold you have chosen. Pack it in very tight. Let dry overnight or put it in the fridge for at least 30 minutes to set.

Student Activities: DIY Activities (cont.)

DIY Stress Ball

Materials:

Latex balloon (NOT a water balloon as this will break too easily)

Funnel

Corn starch

Water

Instructions:

1. Attach the funnel to the balloon.
2. Fill the balloon with a little bit of water to give it some weight.
3. Add about 1 tablespoon of cornstarch and massage the ingredients together in the bottom of the balloon.
4. Continue adding a little bit of water and cornstarch at a time and massaging them together as you go until your balloon is full. You may need to use a slender object like a plastic knife to push the last of the ingredients down into the balloon.
5. Once your balloon is full and you are happy with the consistency of the ingredients inside, remove the funnel and tie the end of the balloon in a knot.

Make Your Own Slime

Materials:

1 cup warm water

½ teaspoon borax

1 bottle of white school glue

Optional – acrylic paint to add color

Instructions:

1. Make the slime activator. In a cup or small bowl, mix 1 cup of warm water with ½ teaspoon of borax until the borax is completely dissolved. Set aside.
2. Pour out the bottle of school glue into a large mixing bowl. If you want to add color, add the desired amount and desired color of acrylic paint.
3. Add the slime activator a little bit at a time to the glue mixture and begin stirring. The mixture will begin to thicken. Continue adding and stirring the slime activator into the glue mixture until the desired consistency is reached.
4. Store in an airtight container.

Student Activities: Other Craft Activities

Watercolor Activity

Materials:

Watercolor palette

Watercolor brush

Cup of water

Paper towel or napkin

Paper (watercolor paper works best but is not necessary)

Instructions:

When using watercolor paint, it is important to use a lot of water. That's why they call it watercolor! Before you begin painting, dip your brush into the cup of water and place a single drop of water on each color of the palette.

To paint, simply wet your brush and dip it into the color you would like to start with, then use your brush to add that color to the page. You also must rinse your brush in the water cup when you are ready to switch colors so that the colors don't get mixed in the palette. One tip for beginners is to lay down the lighter colors that you intend to use on the paper first, and then move on to the darker shades.

For this activity, you can paint anything you want! Use your imagination and get creative. You could paint a simple outdoor scene of a field with a house and a pond. You could paint letters and write an uplifting quote. You could paint your favorite flower or fruit. The options are endless!

Student Activities: Other Craft Activities (cont.)

Hand Tracing

Materials:

Paper

Pen or pencil

Crayons, colored pencils, or gel pens

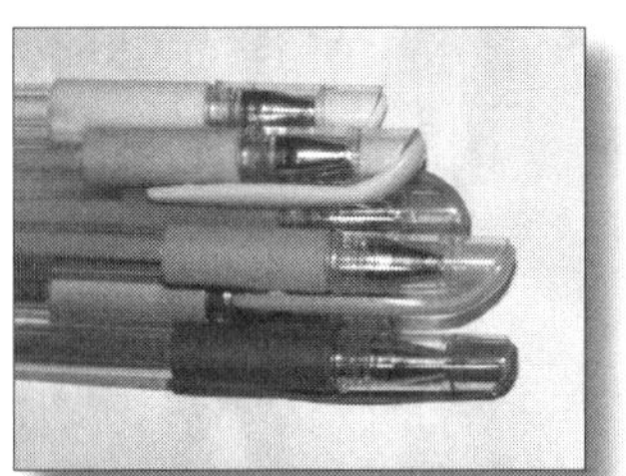

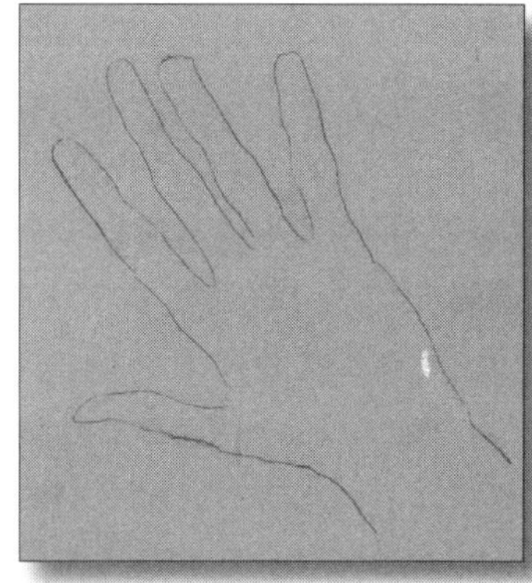

Instructions:

With a piece of paper and a writing utensil, lay your hand flat and trace it. Once that is complete, add patterns or color inside the hand. This will help you to focus on the sensation of the crayon/pencil moving next to your hand, instead of any anxious or overwhelming feelings you may be feeling. Coloring and drawing patterns will also stimulate creativity in your brain to help cope with overwhelming thoughts and feelings.

If you enjoy craft activities and want to try some that are more difficult than the ones provided above, here are some more advanced activities you could try on your own.

Use the internet or another resource (like the local library or someone you know who could help you) to learn how to complete these.

- Knit
- Crochet
- Sew
- DIY weighted blanket

Using Distraction Activities to Cope

Teacher/Parent Introduction

This section mainly focuses on distraction coping mechanisms that can help a child or teenager overcome feelings of anxiety or even a mental breakdown. Most people can admit to having a mental breakdown at least once in their life (kids and teens included!) where it feels like everything is spiraling out of control. Sometimes this can escalate to a panic attack, which is when a person experiences sudden and intense fear or anxiety that is often accompanied with physical symptoms such as increased heart rate, sweating, shortness of breath, chest pain, trembling or shaking, nausea, etc. When this happens, it may be best for your teen to partake in an activity that will cause a distraction so they can think about something else while they calm down. The following page lists some good distraction techniques for your teen to try.

Rearranging Your Bedroom and *Trying Out Minimalism* give your teen physical and mental activities that can provide distractions from stressful situations or thinking. Even if they don't actually rearrange their room or pare down their possessions, the planning can provide a mental break from the stress.

This section also contains different kinds of puzzles that will help energize the brain. Puzzles like these reinforce the connections between brain cells, which leads to overall better brain function. Also, when a puzzle is completed, studies have shown that the brain releases dopamine, which is one of the happy hormones that helps to regulate and improve one's mood. These puzzles are a much better alternative to zoning out with a phone or tablet, and some have even been shown to have the same effect on a person as meditation! Puzzles are an example of distraction and mindfulness coping skills as they help take the mind off what is currently stressing out the person and bring the person's attention back to the present moment.

Student Activities: Stopping a Breakdown in Its Tracks!

Instructions: Have you ever felt like things were spiraling out of control? Sometimes this can escalate to a panic attack, which is when a person experiences sudden and intense fear or anxiety that is often accompanied with physical symptoms such as increased heart rate, sweating, shortness of breath, chest pain, trembling or shaking, nausea, etc. If this ever happens to you, completing an activity as a distraction can help you think about something else while you calm down.

Here are some good distraction techniques to try.

1. Switch your phone to silent mode and put it in a drawer for one hour.

2. Watch a funny movie.

3. Watch an inspiring TED Talk on YouTube.

4. Take a 30-minute nap. Don't forget to set an alarm!

5. Complete one item on your to-do list that you have been ignoring.

6. Watch an episode of your favorite show.

7. Play a game outside.

8. Rearrange your room.

9. Write a short story.

10. Call a friend and ask about their day.

11. Deep clean your bedroom.

12. Take a long bath or shower.

13. Drink a glass of cold water and/or suck on an ice cube.

14. Complete a homework assignment.

15. Complete an activity from this book!

Name: Date:

Student Activities: Rearranging Your Bedroom

Instructions: Sometimes we need a mental reset to cope with difficult times, and rearranging your bedroom is a great way to reset your mind. In the space below, draw a new and improved layout of your room, and carry out the new arrangement when you get home this evening. If you are unable to move the furniture in your room, try rearranging what is on your nightstand, desk, etc.

Name: Date:

Student Activities: Trying Out Minimalism

Instructions: Did you know that your space is often a reflection of your mental state? If you have a cluttered space, you most likely have a cluttered mind; and a cluttered mind is not relaxed or efficient.

1. Pick a space to declutter and turn into a minimalist space. This could be your bedroom, bathroom, locker, desk, or any other space that is yours only (do not get rid of items that are not yours).

2. Now, evaluate the space and each item that is in it. What items are just taking up space but not being used? Put those in a pile to donate to a local church or charity.

3. To take this activity a step further, what items do you have and use but would be completely fine doing without? Set those aside or donate those items as well.

You may be surprised at how much lighter and relieved you feel when you pare down a space that you use regularly to the bare minimum. A decluttered space is a decluttered mind!

Use the space below to make notes or lists of what you want to keep or donate.

____

____

____

____

____

____

____

____

____

Name: _______________________   Date: _______________

Student Activities: Waking Up Your Brain

Word Unscramble

Instructions: Below are mental health terms that need unscrambled. Rearrange the letters to reveal the correct spelling.

1. flsensudmin   _______________________________
2. tduetrgai   _______________________________
3. ixntyae   _______________________________
4. nipgco lkilss   _______________________________
5. tmoosnie   _______________________________
6. teditmnaoi   _______________________________
7. letnam lhhate   _______________________________
8. nspsroeedi   _______________________________
9. nnuirgodg   _______________________________
10. ypeathr   _______________________________
11. nobudaeirs   _______________________________
12. sssert   _______________________________
13. yrrwo   _______________________________
14. nailgnourj   _______________________________
15. iipsoevt knighitn   _______________________________

Name: _______________________________   Date: _______________________

Student Activities: Waking Up Your Brain (cont.)

Word Search

Instructions: Find and circle the words from the word bank in the puzzle. Words can go in any direction and words can share letters as they cross over each other.

ANXIETY	BOUNDARIES	COPING SKILLS
DEPRESSION	EMOTIONS	GRATITUDE
HEALING	HEALTH	MEDICATION
MENTAL	MINDFULNESS	POSITIVE
PSYCHIATRIST	STIGMA	STRESS
SYMPTOM	THERAPIST	THERAPY
THOUGHTS	TRAUMA	TRIGGER
WORRY		

Name: Date:

Student Activities: Waking Up Your Brain (cont.)

Sudoku Puzzles

Instructions: Sudoku is played on a grid of 9 x 9 spaces. Within the rows and columns are 9 squares (outlined in bold and made up of 3 x 3 spaces). Each row, column, and square (9 spaces each) are to be filled with the numbers 1–9, without repeating any numbers within the row, column, or square. For example, the top row already has a 4, so another 4 cannot go in that row; the upper left square already has a 1, so another 1 cannot go in that square, and so on.

The more numbers that are provided to begin with, the easier the puzzle is to solve. The easy level provides the most numbers to begin with, the medium level puzzle provides fewer numbers to begin with, and the hard level puzzle provides the least numbers to begin.

EASY

1			4			2		9
		7						
5	8	9				1		
						3	9	
7					1	5		
	4		6					2
9	6			5				
		5			8			
3	7			2		9	6	

***Hint for beginners** – The number 5 belongs in the bottom right corner of the puzzle. This is so because the bottom right square needs a 5, but there is already a 5 in the seventh and eighth row of the puzzle, so the number 5 cannot go in any other space in the bottom right square. It must go in the bottom right corner of the bottom right square.

Name: ___________________________   Date: ___________________________

Student Activities: Waking Up Your Brain (cont.)

Sudoku Puzzles

MEDIUM

2	9		3	1			4	
4	5		7			9		
	1		6					
				2				
	2		1			4		
6		5	4		7		2	3
1		4	9		3			7
			2					
		2						6

HARD

9				7	6			8
	2							
			2	9				
3				6	4			
		9	3					
	6	8					4	
	8	7						5
		2		4				6
5			9	2			7	

Getting Organized With Goals and Schedules

Teacher/Parent Introduction

The following section will teach the student the basics of goal setting, creating routines, and how to manage their time effectively. The first student activity, *The Importance of Routines and How to Create Them,* will teach the student how to create a morning and evening routine that sets them up for success each day. A consistent daily routine is essential for a reduction in anxiety because it creates a more controlled and predictable environment, and it helps to eliminate decision fatigue. (**Decision fatigue** is the idea that your ability to make decisions worsens over the course of the day because making decision after decision is tiring. The more that you can make your life "automatic," the fewer decisions you will have to make.)

The second student activity, *The Basics of Time Management and How to Make a Daily Schedule,* will help the student become more independent while also reducing their stress levels. When a child learns how to use their time wisely, they will experience decreased feelings of stress and anxiety because they will not be rushed to complete the items on their to-do list. This section will teach the student how to prioritize, how to time-block, and how to utilize a calendar system. This section also includes a *Daily Planner Template* that will prompt the student to list  everything they need to get done and to create a daily schedule that ensures they complete the items on their to-do list. You can encourage your teen in this by leading by example. If you are always running late and missing deadlines, your teen will follow suit. On the contrary, if you are responsible with your time and stay on top of your to-do list, your teen will follow suit.

The third student activity, *How to Set and Achieve Goals,* will guide your teen on how to set reasonable and measurable goals and how to work toward them in an appropriate time frame. *Setting SMART Goals* gives examples of goals that have missed the mark. Students will have the opportunity to devise corrected goals for each situation.

As an influential adult in a teen's life, make sure you are encouraging them to set goals that they want to set, not goals that you think they should set. They will be much more motivated and successful in pursuing goals they set on their own as opposed to goals that are forced on them. You can also help your teen revise their goals to assure they are specific, measurable, and realistic. Setting and working toward goals will encourage them to take initiative and work for the things they want to accomplish in life, and they will soon learn the thrill of achieving as a byproduct. This is followed by the final activity, *How to Make a Vision Board,* which can be a helpful tool when setting out to achieve goals.

Student Activities: The Importance of Routines and How to Create Them

Have you ever thought about what you do to start your day and how that might affect you later in the day? For example, if you have ever overslept and had to rush to get somewhere, you probably felt "off" for the rest of the morning or maybe even the rest of the day. Similarly, have you ever thought about how you end your day? Maybe you stay up too late scrolling on social media or playing video games. As a result, you wake up extremely tired from not getting enough sleep, which causes you to forget your homework at home and impairs your thinking and judgment the entire day. Whatever it is, the way you start and end your day has the ability either to set you up for success or failure. It really is up to you!

It is important to remember that you are in control of how you start and end your day. When you decide to have a balanced and consistent morning and bedtime routine, you will feel more confident and secure because the bookends of your day are predictable and familiar. Consistent routines also promote mental sharpness, emotional well-being, better energy levels, and they help to eliminate potential **decision fatigue**, or making poorer decisions thoughout the day because you get tired of making decisions. This section will help you figure out what works for you and will teach you how to turn this into a process that does not require much thought. This will free up your mind for the more important things in life.

Bedtime and Morning Routines

A good morning begins the night before, so it is actually important to implement a good nighttime routine first. A good bedtime routine sets you up for success in the morning and ensures a night of restful sleep. Listed below are several ideas for things you can do before bed as a part of your bedtime routine. Start simple by just picking a few activities to complete each night, and feel free to add more activities as you get the hang of it.

Bedtime routine ideas:

- Pack up all schoolwork.
- Pack your lunch if you do not want to eat school lunch.
- Look up tomorrow's weather and pick out what you plan to wear.
- Avoid screens in the last hour before bedtime as being on screens can make it harder to fall asleep and stay asleep.
- Take care of your personal hygiene by brushing your teeth, taking a shower, etc.
- Do something relaxing to help you wind down—read a book, do yoga, listen to calm music, meditate, journal, etc.

Student Activities: The Importance of Routines and How to Create Them (cont.)

- Tidy bedroom and desk area.
- Change into pajamas.
- Set an alarm that allows plenty of time in the morning. If using your phone, try keeping it across the room or in a different room entirely so you have to get out of bed to turn it off.
- Make a to-do list for the next day.

Other tips to help you get a good night of sleep include creating a soothing sleep environment with cool temperatures, a fluffy pillow and blanket, a sound machine, no screens, etc.; keeping a regular sleep schedule by going to bed at or around the same time every night, even on the weekends; and going to bed early enough to allow for 9–11 hours of sleep.

Now that you have had a restful night's sleep, you can tackle a healthy morning routine that will ensure you are ready to take on whatever comes each day. Listed below are several activities you can do to start your day. Again, start simple by just committing to a few activities, and feel free to add more as you see fit.

Morning routine ideas:
- Wake up at or around the same time each day, even on the weekends.
- Don't hit snooze! Keeping your alarm out of reach so you have to get our of your bed to turn it off will help with this.
- Meditate.
- Make a list of gratitudes.
- Take care of your personal hygiene by brushing your teeth, taking a shower, etc.
- Get dressed and put away pajamas.
- Make the bed.
- Go for a light walk.
- Eat a high protein breakfast (protein keeps you full for a longer period of time and will give you ample amounts of energy to start your day).
  - On the contrary, avoid sugary breakfast items because you will be hungry sooner and will experience a sugar crash mid-morning.
- Listen to positive/uplifting music.
- Review the day's schedule and to-do list, or make one if you have not already.
- Drink water to help wake up your brain and bodily organs.
- Double-check bookbag (and lunch box) and pack everything you need for the day.
- Leave with plenty of time.

Name: | Date:

Student Activities: The Importance of Routines and How to Create Them (cont.)

My Routines

Instructions: Pulling inspiration from the lists on the previous pages, use the space provided to create your own bedtime and morning routine.

My Bedtime Routine

My Morning Routine

Student Activities: The Basics of Time Management and How to Create a Daily Schedule

This section will teach you how to manage your time wisely and why it is important to do so. Time management is an essential life skill that reduces feelings of frustration and overwhelm, while also increasing independence, productivity levels, and your ability to focus. You will experience more time freedom and a sense of calm knowing that you have time to do what you *want* to do when you stick to the schedule outlining what you *need* to do. Managing time effectively and efficiently will also improve your performance at school, work, and extracurricular activities. Time management skills are good to practice now, even if you are not overly busy yet, so that when extracurriculars and jobs enter your life, you are already armed with this valuable life skill.

Helpful tips for successful time management:

- Set limits on your electronic devices, especially social media apps. These are time-sucking vortexes that steal your time without you even noticing!
- Avoid multitasking. It is always a better option to give one task 100% of your attention and effort than to give two things less than 100% of your attention and effort.
- Learn how to prioritize your tasks. You will need to discern what needs to be done immediately, what can be scheduled for later, what you can delegate to someone else, and what you can delete from your to-do list entirely.
  - Do immediately: Important tasks with defined deadlines, or ones you have put off for so long that they are now overdue.
  - Schedule for later: Important tasks with no defined deadlines.
  - Delegate: Tasks that someone else can do.
  - Delete: Tasks you can eliminate because they are not critical to your goals or mission.
- Complete the most difficult task first. Sometimes, when you begin by completing the item that is causing you the most stress or that requires the most of your mental energy, you will be more efficient as you continue to work.
  - Some of the time, the opposite of this may be more beneficial to you. You may find that completing small and quick tasks first gets you on a roll to keep working and stay focused.
- Batch similar items together. For example, if you need to do three different chores and two homework assignments, you will be more efficient if you complete all the chores at once and then all the homework assignments at once, instead of switching back and forth between homework and chores.
- When you plan out what you want to complete each day, be sure to set reasonable time limits for items on your to-do list. Do not think that you can complete all the week's homework in one hour, or that you can complete the day's chores in five minutes.

Student Activities: The Basics of Time Management and How to Create a Daily Schedule (cont.)

- Stay organized by keeping a neat desk/workspace so you do not have to spend time looking for the items needed to complete your homework.
- Set timers to help you stay on task. For example, if you have one hour to work on homework before sports practice, set a timer for one hour so that you don't have to keep checking the clock to prevent being late. You will know that you can work until you hear your alarm go off and you will still be on time to practice.
- Remember that plans change. Do not fill your schedule so full that there is no room for flexibility. This is not realistic and will not set you up for success.

The following activity will encourage you to spend your time more efficiently by prompting you to make a to-do list and plan out when you will complete the items on your list. Having a plan for your day will reduce your stress when you can literally see that you have enough time to get everything done that needs to be done. This being the age of technology, you can also use the calendar app on your phone to schedule out your day's tasks. Planning out your days is the key to achieving short and long-term goals, as this will help you stay focused and overcome the distractions that are all around you.

Instructions: Use the *Daily Planner Template (Example)* as a guide to fill out your own daily planner. Make several copies of the *Daily Planner Template.* Try filling out the planner for one day and seeing how well you can stay on schedule. Next, increase to two or three days of planners, and then try filling out daily planners for a whole week. Compare how well you are staying on schedule and how you are feeling when you are using the planners to when you aren't using them.

Name: ______________________   Date: ______________

Student Activities: Daily Planner Template (Example)

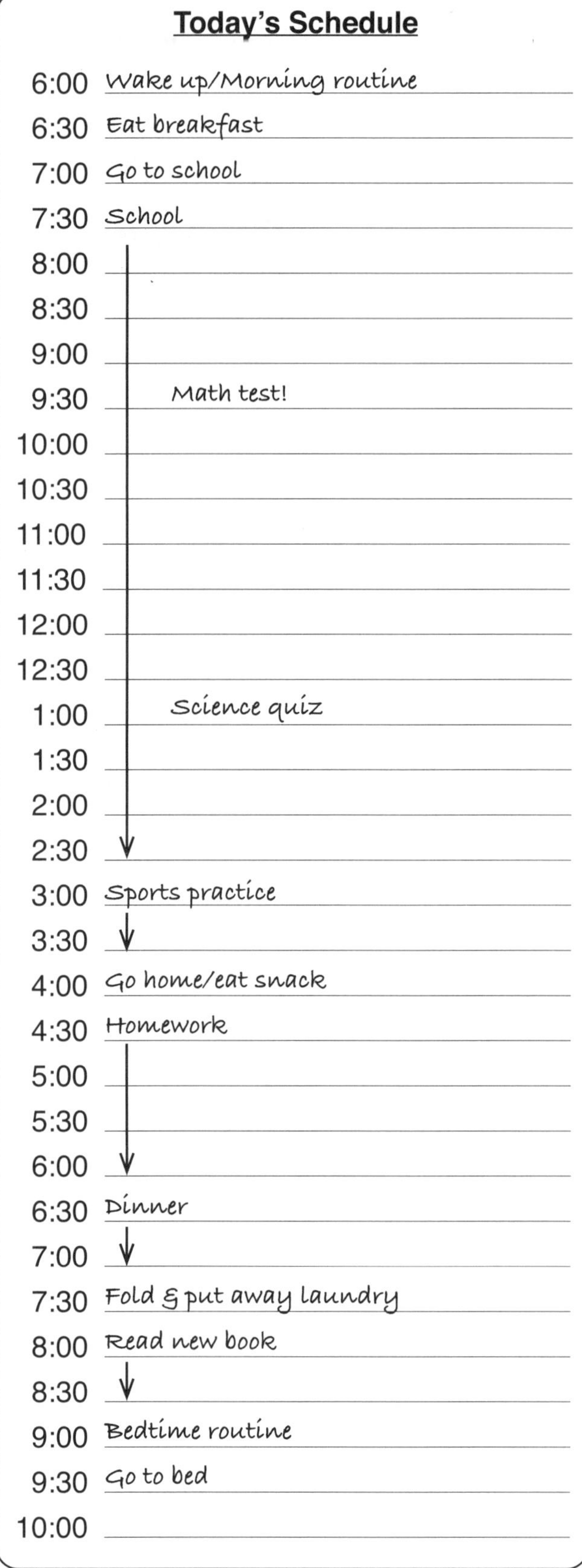

Today's Schedule

6:00	Wake up/Morning routine
6:30	Eat breakfast
7:00	Go to school
7:30	School
8:00	
8:30	
9:00	
9:30	Math test!
10:00	
10:30	
11:00	
11:30	
12:00	
12:30	
1:00	Science quiz
1:30	
2:00	
2:30	
3:00	Sports practice
3:30	
4:00	Go home/eat snack
4:30	Homework
5:00	
5:30	
6:00	
6:30	Dinner
7:00	
7:30	Fold & put away laundry
8:00	Read new book
8:30	
9:00	Bedtime routine
9:30	Go to bed
10:00	

Today's Big Three

1. Review for math test and science quiz before school
2. Today's chores (laundry)
3. Work on English paper

To-Do List

- ❑ Pick out tomorrow's clothes
- ❑ Pick new book to read
- ❑ Complete homework
- ❑ Do something nice for someone
- ❑
- ❑
- ❑
- ❑
- ❑
- ❑
- ❑
- ❑
- ❑
- ❑
- ❑
- ❑

Daily Gratitude

I am thankful for a bed to sleep in at night.

Name:

Date:

Student Activities: Daily Planner Template

Today's Schedule

6:00
6:30
7:00
7:30
8:00
8:30
9:00
9:30
10:00
10:30
11:00
11:30
12:00
12:30
1:00
1:30
2:00
2:30
3:00
3:30
4:00
4:30
5:00
5:30
6:00
6:30
7:00
7:30
8:00
8:30
9:00
9:30
10:00

Today's Big Three

1.
2.
3.

To-Do List

❏
❏
❏
❏
❏
❏
❏
❏
❏
❏
❏
❏
❏
❏
❏
❏

Daily Gratitude

Student Activities: How to Set and Achieve Goals

As a young person, you have a lifetime ahead of you that is full of opportunities to set and accomplish goals. The time will pass anyway, so you might as well spend that time working toward something you are passionate about! Your goals can be academic, personal, or professional. Whatever kind of goal you decide to set, it is important to be passionate about it and know your "why" behind the goal, as this will help you stay motivated to achieve it. Ask yourself, "Why is this goal important and valuable to me? How will achieving this goal benefit my life?"

Henry Ford famously said, "Whether you think you can or you can't, you're right." This means that when you set out to accomplish something, mindset is everything. If you truly believe that you can do something, you can! And if you are convinced than you cannot do something, you will most likely fail. Doubt kills more dreams than failure ever will.

A helpful guide to setting goals that you are sure to achieve is called **SMART goals**.

Specific – your goal should be clear and well-defined.

Measurable – your goal should include precise dates, amounts, etc. This will help you know when you have successfully met your goal.

Attainable – your goal should be realistic. Unrealistic goals will diminish your confidence and keep you from setting other goals. If you've never set and achieved a goal before, it might be a good idea to start with setting a short-term goal like running one mile, before you set out to achieve a long-term goal like training for a marathon.

Relevant to the direction you want your life to take. This could be an important time to reflect on the kind of person you want to be and what goals you can set to become that kind of person.

Time-bound – your goal must have a deadline, or it can drag on so long that you will lose motivation.

In addition to using the SMART goal guide, you should put your goal in writing and post it somewhere that you will see it often. Write down the goal in big letters at the top, followed by the necessary steps you must take to achieve the goal. You can also write these smaller steps in your daily schedule to make sure you are working toward your goal each day. Cross each step off as you achieve them to track your progress and keep you motivated.

You may be thinking, what happens if you set a goal, work toward it, but ultimately fail? In that case, you have then learned how to stick with something and how to set and work toward a goal. It is only considered a failure if you fall down and stay down. If you do not accomplish what you set out to accomplish, dust yourself off and try again.

Name: _______________________________   Date: _______________

Student Activities: How to Set and Achieve Goals (cont.)

Instructions: Take some time and brainstorm some goals that you might like to set in the near or distant future. Here are some ideas to get you thinking…

- Earn and save a certain amount of money to buy something for yourself or a loved one.
- Learn how to change a flat tire.
- Make student council.
- Make a sports team.
- Be invited to join the National Honor Society.
- Train for and run a 5K.

____

____

____

____

____

____

____

____

____

____

____

____

____

____

____

Name: _______________________   Date: _______________________

Student Activities: Setting SMART Goals

Instructions: Listed below are multiple goals that have something wrong with them. Using the SMART goal guide, identify what is wrong with each goal. Then, rewrite the goal so that it follows the SMART goal guide. The first one is partially done for you.

1. Train for a marathon by this Saturday.

   Answer: This goal is not attainable. It is not realistic to train for a marathon in under a week.

   Corrected goal: ____

   ____

2. Save money by January 1.

   Answer: ____

   ____

   Corrected goal: ____

   ____

3. Write a book by the time I am 30 years old.

   Answer: ____

   ____

   Corrected goal: ____

   ____

4. Learn how to change a flat tire on my dad's Honda Civic with my dad.

   Answer: ____

   ____

   Corrected goal: ____

   ____

5. Make a sports team this school year by practicing three days a week after school.

   Answer: ____

   ____

   Corrected goal: ____

   ____

Name: _______________________   Date: _______________________

Student Activities: How to Make a Vision Board

Instructions: Use magazines, the Internet, or other image sources to cut out and gather images that remind you of and inspire you to achieve your goal. (Make sure you have permission to cut pictures from these sources.) Fix these images to your vision board and place it somewhere you will see it often.

Example for the goal – I want to train and run in a 5K.

My vision board for the goal – ____

Getting Active by Grounding and Exercising

Teacher/Parent Introduction

Grounding is a common and effective coping skill used to make it through difficult times. Grounding is a method of self-soothing that helps bring you into the present moment and overcome the feelings of stress and anxiety that accompany a bad day or difficult situation. It can also be used to bring one back to reality after a panic attack or PTSD flashback. When you focus on your current surroundings, you will begin to realize that you are safe, and you will begin to feel calmer. Grounding can take many different forms and can be done indoors and outdoors. The first student section, *Grounding Yourself Indoors,* contains eight different exercises to help the student put the concept into practice indoors.

The second student section, *Grounding Yourself Outdoors,* contains ten different exercises and activities to help the student put the concept of grounding into practice outdoors. Spending

time outside is crucial because studies have shown that spending time outside, especially barefoot, has mental and physical health benefits such as reducing inflammation in the body, improving sleep, increasing energy levels, lowering stress levels, promoting calmness, and relieving muscle tension. Many sources recommend spending at least 20 minutes a day barefoot outside to reap these benefits.

The final student section, *Let's Get Moving,* prompts the student to participate in simple exercise. It is recommended that teens get at least 60 minutes of physical activity per day for optimal health. Not only is exercise beneficial to one's physical health by helping prevent heart disease, type 2 diabetes, and unhealthy weight gain, it has also been proven to have a strong, positive impact on one's mental health. For example, physical activity releases **endorphins** (one of the four "happy hormones"), which helps fight anxiety and depression and helps one manage stress.

Student Activities: Grounding Yourself Indoors

Instructions: Complete the following activities indoors to help you practice **grounding**—a common coping skill used to bring you into the present moment and overcome feelings of stress and anxiety.

1. Reorient yourself in the moment when you are feeling anxious by answering the following questions on your own sheet of paper.

   a. My name is…

   b. My age is…

   c. I live in…

   d. My eyes are…

   e. My hair is…

   f. Today is…

   g. My favorite color is…

   h. My favorite food is…

   i. My shirt is…

2. Release muscle tension by stretching with or without a partner. Below are simple stretches to help get you started, but you can also look on the internet for more advanced stretches or yoga exercises. Stretching not only releases physical tension in the body, it also helps you feel more relaxed and uplifted by increasing **serotonin** levels (one of the body's four "happy hormones").

   a. With your feet a couple feet apart, reach up as high up to the sky as you can all the way through your fingertips. With your arms still reaching up, lean your torso to the right and then to the left, holding the stretch on each side for 10 seconds. Keeping your legs straight, bend at the waist and touch the floor if you can. If you cannot touch the floor, bend down as far as you can and let your arms and head hang down. Hold this position for 10 seconds.

   b. Now sit on the floor with your feet straight out in front of you. Reach forward as far as you can and try to touch your toes. Hold this position for 10 seconds. Staying on the floor, spread your legs as far apart as is comfortable. With both legs straight, reach toward your right leg and try to touch your toes for 10 seconds. Then repeat on the left side for 10 seconds.

   c. Now lie flat on your back and, keeping your left leg straight, hug your right leg into your chest for 10 seconds. Repeat on the other side by keeping your right leg straight and hugging your left leg into your chest for 10 seconds. Next, keeping your right leg straight, stretch your left leg across your body to the right side for 10 seconds. Repeat this on the other side by straightening your left leg and stretching your right leg across the left side of your body for 10 seconds.

Student Activities: Grounding Yourself Indoors (cont.)

3. Deep breathing can help slow a racing heart and mind and has been clinically proven to reduce anxiety and tension in the body. Use the 4-4-4 method while breathing as deeply as you can. Breathe in through your nose for 4 seconds, hold your breath for 4 seconds, and blow out through your mouth for 4 seconds. Repeat this as long as necessary.

4. The 3-3-3 rule has also been effective in helping children and adolescents cope with feelings of stress and anxiety. All it takes is looking around and naming 3 things you see, then naming 3 things you hear, then moving 3 different parts of your body (for example, your ankle, finger, and shoulder).

5. Yoga is an activity that focuses on breathing, stretching, and relaxing—all things that help reduce feelings of anxiety. Below are two different YouTube videos that you can follow along with to practice yoga. The first video is only 5 minutes long and is for beginners. The second video is 20 minutes long and is a little more advanced than the first, but still doable for teens.

   The first video is titled "5 Minute Easy and Relaxing Yoga for Anxiety" and can be found on the YouTube channel "The Partnership in Education."
   <https://www.youtube.com/watch?v=q3ZkuwabZyQ>

   The second video is titled "Yoga For Teens | Yoga With Adriene" and can be found on the "Yoga with Adriene" YouTube channel.
   <https://www.youtube.com/watch?v=7kgZnJqzNaU>

6. Body scan – Sit somewhere comfortably and close your eyes. Take a few deep belly breaths and clear your mind. Now, notice how your body feels. Starting at the top of your head and working your way down through every part of your body, take a mental note as to how you are feeling physically. What feels comfortable? What feels uncomfortable? Are you sitting on something hard or soft? Is any part of you hot or cold? Make as many observations as you can as you do your body scan.

7. Watch **autonomous sensory meridian response (ASMR)** videos. ASMR is a relaxing feeling that overcomes someone in response to a certain stimulus. There are many different types of ASMR videos that you may like, and you can find these through a simple search on Google or YouTube.

8. Recite something in order. For example, you could multiply by 3s, say the alphabet backwards, recite something you have memorized such as Scripture or poetry. You can write these things down if that helps you keep your mind from wandering.

Student Activities: Grounding Yourself Outdoors

Instructions: Complete the following activities outdoors to help you practice **grounding**—a common coping skill used to bring you into the present moment and overcome feelings of stress and anxiety. (Avoid dangerous areas and poisonous or harmful plants and substances when touching or tasting items.)

1. Lie in the grass and make shapes out of the clouds overhead. If it is dark outside, look for star constellations or make your own shapes out of the stars. You can also do this with a partner to see if you are both thinking of the same thing. Notice the feeling of the grass against your skin—does it feel soft? Prickly? Notice the feel of the air around you—is it windy? Hot, cold, or just right? Notice the smell of the air around you—do you smell anything in particular? Does it smell pleasant or unpleasant?

2. Go outside and find 5 different types of leaves. Use the internet or another resource to identify what kinds of trees or plants these leaves came from.

3. Implement the A B C method. Go outside and find something that begins with each letter of the alphabet. Record your findings on your own sheet of paper.

4. Implement the 5 4 3 2 1 method. Find 5 things you can see, 4 things you can touch, 3 things you can hear, 2 things you can smell, and 1 thing you can taste.

5. Go for a walk barefoot outside and make the following observations:
   a. How does the ground feel against my feet?
   b. Is there a breeze blowing?
   c. Am I feeling warm, chilly, or just right?
   d. What sounds do I hear?
   e. What can I smell?

6. Gardening and yardwork can also be a great way to practice grounding. This could be pulling weeds, planting seeds that will grow into flowers or food, transplanting flowers that have already sprouted, raking leaves, mowing the lawn, etc. Choose one of these to complete outside at your home or with your classmates at school. While you are completing your chosen gardening activity, make an intentional effort to be aware of your surroundings and how you are feeling in the moment. How does the soil feel? How is the weather? What do you see? Hear? How are you feeling in this moment?

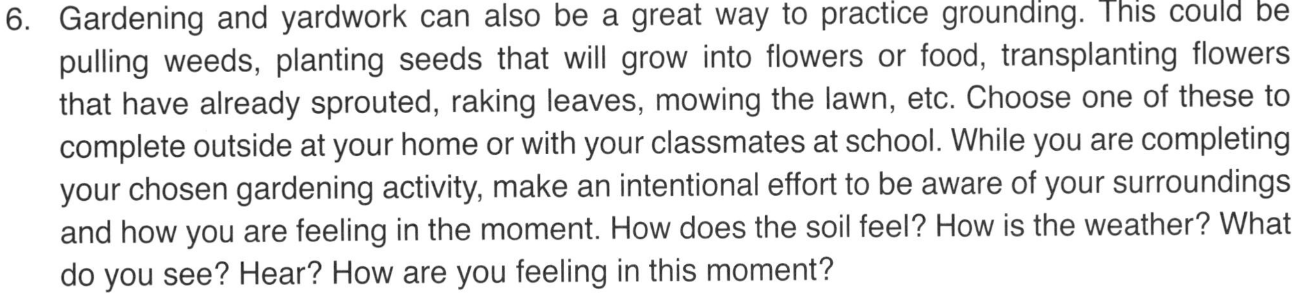

Student Activities: Grounding Yourself Outdoors (cont.)

7. If it is currently winter where you live, there are plenty of ways you can practice grounding outside. Remember, there is no such thing as bad weather, only bad clothing. Bundle up and get outside! Some winter outdoor activities include shoveling snow, building a snowman, making snow angels, and going on nature walks.

8. Sprints – Run as fast as you can for 30 seconds. Do this two to three times while timing yourself. This activity will increase blood flow to your brain and other organs, which will help you stay focused and think clearly. Exercising also releases **endorphins**, a hormone in your body that causes you to feel happy. This activity can also be completed with a partner by timing each other and taking turns completing your sprints while the other catches their breath.

9. Sound identification – With a partner, find a place to sit outside with a piece of paper and something to write with. Identify as many sounds as you can and write them down. Do this for at least 10 minutes. When the time is up, compare your list of identified sounds with your partner. Do you both have the same sounds listed? Did they notice more or less than you?

10. Using the internet or another resource, find a map of common star constellations that are visible from your location. On a clear night, lie down outside and look up at the stars. Try to locate as many constellations as you can. To take this a step further, try to come up with your own constellations. Do you see any shapes in the stars that are not already named constellations?

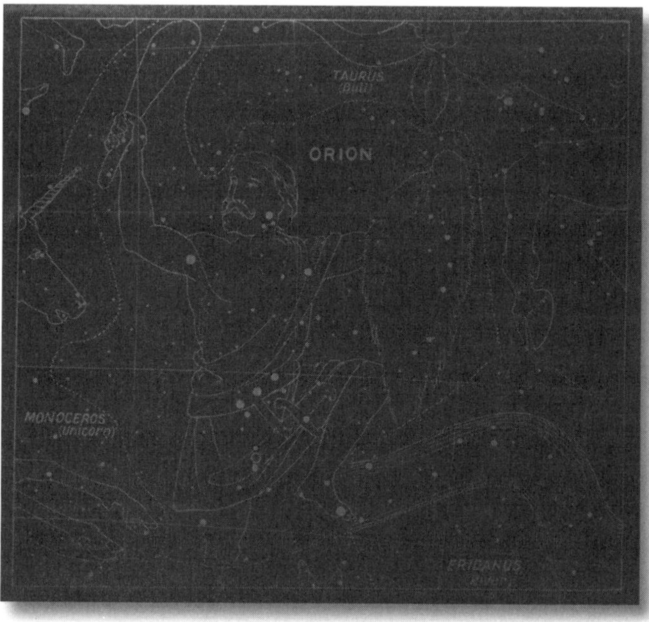

Name: Date:

Student Activities: Let's Get Moving

Exercise can always be done alone but is often more fun with a friend. Listed below are some physical activities that may interest you and be a fun way to get moving.

Instructions: Read through the lists and think about which activities you already enjoy and/or which activities you would like to try!

- Going for a walk with a pet, family member, friend, or just yourself
- Yoga or Pilates
- Yard work like raking leaves or gardening
- Rock climbing
- Hunting/fishing
- Horseback riding
- Jumping on a trampoline
- Disc golf
- Riding your bike
- Playing on a playground
- Roller skating
- Jumping rope
- Hitting balls at the batting cages
- Nature hikes
- Tag games
- Kayaking or canoeing
- Surfing
- Video games that encourage physical activity (for example, Wii Sports or Just Dance)
- Even playing putt putt golf gets you up and moving!

You may also be interested in organized team and/or individual sports through school or local clubs, which could include:

• Baseball	• Track and field
• Football	• Tennis
• Soccer	• Golf
• Dance	• Wrestling
• Basketball	• Gymnastics
• Volleyball	• Skateboarding
• Lacrosse	• Bodybuilding
• Hockey	• Snow or water skiing
• Water polo	• Swimming
• Crew	• Martial arts

Name: _______________________   Date: _______________

Student Activities: Let's Get Moving (cont.)

Instructions: Use the space below to list all the activities that you are interested in. Then, plan ways you can incorporate exercise into your daily routine and if you would rather do this alone or with a friend.

I am interested in… ____

____

____

____

____

Ways I can take part in the above listed activities… ________________________

____

____

____

____

____

____

____

____

____

Preparing Recipes for Food and Science

Teacher/Parent Introduction

This section of student activities includes basic cooking recipes and simple science experiments. Cooking can offer many benefits to one's physical and mental health. You can choose

to cook healthy meals with whole foods, which will benefit your physical health. Further, when you take care of your physical health, your mental health also benefits. Cooking food for yourself encourages creativity and can leave you feeling proud of what you have created and provided for yourself and/ or others, thereby increasing your self-esteem and promoting togetherness. Cooking is relaxing for a lot of people, as it engages the senses, especially the sense of smell, which has the power to remind one of positive memories and promote feelings of nostalgia and happiness. It requires focus and attention to detail, which can calm a racing mind. It has also been shown to release the four "happy hormones" in a person's brain—endorphins, oxytocin, serotonin, and dopamine—which all leave a person feeling joy and pleasure. Considering all these factors, cooking has been shown to relieve stress and decrease feelings of depression and anxiety.

The final section of student activities in this book contains science experiments that can be completed easily in a classroom or home setting. Similar to cooking, partaking in these fun and easy science experiments can encourage creativity, engage the senses, and encourage one to focus and pay attention to detail. These factors all contribute to mental health by decreasing

feelings of anxiety and depression and encouraging mindfulness. Completing these science experiments is also a good way for the student to practice a distraction coping skill. While simply distracting oneself is not always the most effective way to deal with stressful situations, it can help to calm a racing mind and allow time to come back to the situation later with a fresh and clear way of thinking.

Student Activities: Basic Recipes

Yogurt Parfait

Ingredients:
Yogurt of choice
- Any type of plain or flavored yogurt

Crunchy item of choice
- Any flavor of granola
- Chia seeds
- Graham cracker

Fruit of choice
- Strawberries
- Raspberries
- Blueberries
- Or any other fruit you enjoy!

Directions:
1. Add the desired amount of yogurt to your bowl or cup.
2. Add any amount of your desired crunchy item and fruit choice.

As you can see, this recipe is very customizable. You can begin with any yogurt base, add an item for crunch and a refreshing fruit item, and you have a delicious yogurt parfait ready in minutes!

Snickerdoodle in a Mug

Ingredients:

For cake mix:
1/4 cup flour
2 tbsp. sugar
1/4 tsp. baking powder
1/4 cup milk
2 tbsp. butter
1/2 tsp. vanilla
1/4 tsp. cinnamon

For topping:
1 tbsp sugar
1/4 tsp cinnamon

Directions:
1. Mix mug cake ingredients in a separate bowl.
2. Layer spoonfuls of cake mix into a mug, and sprinkle topping in between layers.
3. Add the rest of the topping and cook in the microwave for 1–2 minutes on high.
4. Allow this to cool for a few minutes before enjoying!

Student Activities: Basic Recipes (cont.)

Sweet Bread Loaf

Ingredients:

3 cups self-rising flour, sifted

¼ cup white sugar

1 packet of dry active yeast

12 oz. can of ginger ale

2 tbsp. melted butter

Directions:

1. Preheat oven to 375 degrees Fahrenheit.
2. Grease a loaf pan with shortening or spray with cooking spray.
3. In a large mixing bowl, combine all the ingredients (except the butter) and mix by hand with a fork or spoon. (Using an electric mixer can over-mix this batter. It's normal for it to be a little lumpy.)
4. Spread the dough evenly into the greased loaf pan.
5. Pour the melted butter on top of the dough. This will make for a golden-brown crust while baking.
6. Bake in the oven at 375 degrees for 60 minutes.
7. Allow to cool for 15 minutes before cutting into the bread.

Apple Cinnamon Butter

Ingredients:

1/2 cup softened butter

2 tbsp. honey

1 tsp. apple pie spice

1/3 cup powdered sugar

Directions:

1. Blend ingredients together in a small bowl one at a time until thoroughly mixed. A hand mixer may make this easier but is not mandatory.
2. Cover with plastic wrap or a lid and let sit for at least 2 hours. This will allow the flavors time to marry.
3. Serve with muffins, pancakes, or the sweet bread loaf from above!
4. Refrigerate any leftovers.

Student Activities: Basic Recipes (cont.)

Taco Salad

Ingredients:

1 lb. lean ground beef

1 packet taco seasoning

1 head of iceberg lettuce, cut into small pieces
     or shredded

Shredded carrots

Shredded cabbage

Shredded Mexican cheese blend and/or queso

Salsa

Guacamole

Corn

Black beans

Sour cream

Quinoa

Tortilla chips

Directions:

1. In a large skillet over medium heat, brown the ground beef. Drain the fat from the beef and return the beef to the skillet.
2. Add taco seasoning to the beef with the amount of water recommended on the seasoning packet, and follow the directions on the back of the seasoning packet.
3. Add the desired amount of taco meat to your plate with lettuce and any of the other listed ingredients you may like.

This recipe is also quite customizable. Try it with different meats such as ground turkey, shredded pork, fish, or shrimp. You can also use vegetarian options. Many of the toppings listed are optional and allow you to have a lot of variety with one dish.

Student Activities: At-home Science Experiments

Bouncy Egg

Materials:

Jar with lid

Vinegar

Egg

Instructions:

1. Pour some vinegar into the jar. Make sure there is enough to cover the egg.
2. Place the egg in the jar and secure it with the lid.
3. Let sit for 1–2 days. The eggshell should start to fizz over time and will eventually dissolve under the vinegar.
4. Remove the egg from the jar and gently rub away the remaining shell pieces. If the shell is not rubbing off easily, you may try rinsing the egg in cold water while you rub at the shell.
5. After the shell has been completely removed, try dropping the egg from a few inches in the air on a hard and flat surface. And voila, you have a bouncy egg!

Soda Explosion

Materials:

2 liter of Diet Coke

1 roll of Mentos mints

Instructions:

1. Set the 2 liter of Diet Coke on a flat surface in a large open area (preferably outside, as this can be very messy).
2. Unscrew the lid from the soda and set aside.
3. Tear off one end of the Mentos wrapper, leaving the Mentos in the wrapper.
4. Line up the tube of Mentos with the top of the open soda bottle. Carefully and quickly, drop multiple Mentos into the soda and quickly back away to watch the reaction. The more Mentos you can drop into the soda, the bigger the reaction will be.

Student Activities: At-home Science Experiments (cont.)

Elephant Toothpaste

Materials:

Latex gloves   Glass beaker

20% hydrogen peroxide   Dish soap

Food coloring

Potassium iodide (can be found at
          Walmart, Walgreens, CVS, etc.)

Instructions:

1. Set the glass beaker on a large piece of cardboard or trash bag to make for an easy cleanup.
2. Pour the hydrogen peroxide into the glass beaker.
3. Add dish soap.
4. Add food coloring. You can add more than one color for a more colorful reaction.
5. Add the potassium iodide and stand back as you watch the reaction happen!

Mold Science

Materials:

3 baggies   3 bread slices

Hand sanitizer   Hand soap and water

Warm location

Instructions:

1. The purpose of this experiment is to determine the rate at which mold grows on bread that has been handled with dirty hands, hands that have been cleaned with hand sanitizer, and hands that have been cleaned with soap and hot water. Take your three baggies and label them as such: dirty hands, hand sanitizer, and soap and water.
2. Handle the first slice of bread with hands that have not been washed or sanitized in any way. Make sure to touch the bread all over. Now place that piece of bread in its own labeled baggie.
3. Now use hand sanitizer on your hands. Touch a new slice of bread all over and place it in its own labeled baggie.
4. Now wash your hands for at least 30 seconds with hot soapy water. Touch a new slice of bread all over and place it in its own labeled baggie.
5. Finally, hang all the baggies using tape in a warm location. This could be in a window that gets sun every day, or in a warm, interior closet. Your chosen location needs to be warm, or the mold will grow very slowly.
6. Watch daily and document any growth. Hopefully this will motivate you to have good hand hygiene!

Name: Date:

Reflection Activity

As you come to the end of this book, it is time to think back on all the activities that you have spent time completing. Some of the activities probably interested you more than others.

Instructions: Take time below to write down some of the activities you liked and ones you didn't like. What interested you about the activities you liked? Why do you think other activities didn't click with you as well? Further, reflect on what you have learned and why you believe coping skills are important.

Activities I liked and why – ____

____

____

____

____

Activities I didn't like and why – ____

____

____

____

____

What I learned through completing this book – _______________________________

____

____

____

____

Why I believe coping skills are important – _________________________________

____

____

____

____

Motivational Quotes

Instructions: Listed below and on the next page are motivational quotes you can use to help inspire you to dream big, set goals, and persevere through tough times. You can cut out the quotes and keep them in your notebook or post them in your locker, in your bedroom, on your bathroom mirror, etc. If you want, add color and designs to the quotes with crayons or colored pencils.

IT DOES NOT MATTER HOW SLOWLY YOU GO AS LONG AS YOU DO NOT STOP.

–Confucius

The secret of getting ahead is getting started.

–Mark Twain

Optimism is the faith that leads to achievement. Nothing can be done without hope and confidence.

–Helen Keller

If you can dream it, you can do it.

–Walt Disney

You will never win if you never begin.

–Helen Rowland

What you get by achieving your goals is not as important as what you become by achieving your goals.

–Zig Ziglar

Motivational Quotes (cont.)

Our greatest weakness lies in giving up.
The most certain way to succeed is to
always try just one more time.

–Thomas A. Edison

You can do anything,
but not everything.

–David Allen

Don't let someone else's opinion
of you become your reality.

–Les Brown

Setting goals is the first step in turning
the invisible into the visible.

–Tony Robbins

Just one small positive thought in the morning
can change your whole day.

–Dalai Lama

The greatest discovery of my generation is that a
human being can alter his life by altering his attitudes.

–William James

Answer Key

Waking Up Your Brain
Word Unscramble (page 26)

1. Mindfulness
2. Gratitude
3. Anxiety
4. Coping skills
5. Emotions
6. Meditation
7. Mental health
8. Depression
9. Grounding
10. Therapy
11. Boundaries
12. Stress
13. Worry
14. Journaling
15. Positive thinking

Word Search (page 27)

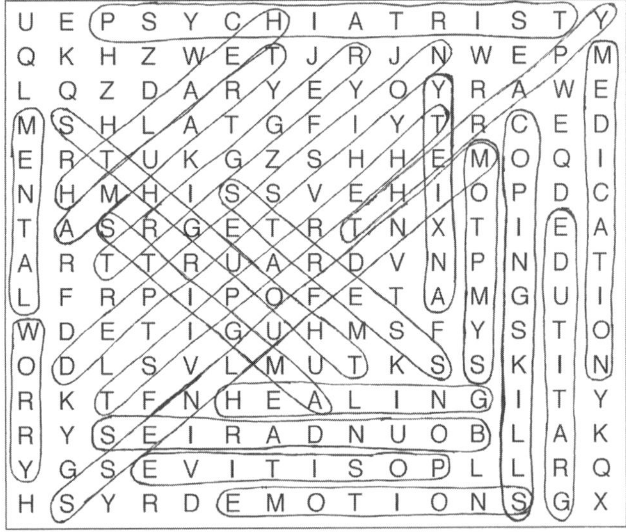

Sudoku Puzzles: Easy (page 28)

1	3	6	4	8	7	2	5	9
4	2	7	5	1	9	6	3	8
5	8	9	2	3	6	1	4	7
6	5	1	8	7	2	3	9	4
7	9	2	3	4	1	5	8	6
8	4	3	6	9	5	7	1	2
9	6	4	7	5	3	8	2	1
2	1	5	9	6	8	4	7	3
3	7	8	1	2	4	9	6	5

Sudoku Puzzles: Medium (page 29)

2	9	7	3	1	5	6	4	8
4	5	6	7	8	2	9	3	1
8	1	3	6	4	9	7	5	2
3	4	1	5	2	6	8	7	9
7	2	9	1	3	8	4	6	5
6	8	5	4	9	7	1	2	3
1	6	4	9	5	3	2	8	7
5	7	8	2	6	1	3	9	4
9	3	2	8	7	4	5	1	6

Sudoku Puzzles: Hard (page 29)

9	1	3	4	7	6	5	2	8
6	2	4	8	3	5	7	1	9
8	7	5	2	9	1	4	6	3
3	5	1	7	6	4	9	8	2
7	4	9	3	8	2	6	5	1
2	6	8	1	5	9	3	4	7
4	8	7	6	1	3	2	9	5
1	9	2	5	4	7	8	3	6
5	3	6	9	2	8	1	7	4

Answer Key (cont.)

How to Set and Achieve Goals
Setting SMART Goals (page 40)

(The corrected goals will vary.)

1. Answer: This goal is not attainable. It is not realistic to train for a marathon in under a week.
2. Answer: This goal is not specific or measurable. An amount should be included, and it would be helpful to say why you want to save the money.
3. Answer: This goal is not specific, and the deadline is too far in the future. Both will cause you to lose motivation.
4. Answer: This goal is specific, measurable, and attainable, but there is no deadline. Every goal should be time-bound.
5. Answer: This goal is not specific enough and should include the exact sport that the student is interested in trying out for.

Bibliography

"The benefit of puzzles for the brain.", Progress Lifeline. (2023) <https://www.progresslifeline.org.uk/news/the-benefit-of-puzzles-for-the-brain#:~:text=Working%20on%20a%20puzzle%20reinforces,to%20improve%20short%2Dterm%20memory.&text=Puzzles%20increase%20the%20production%20of,as%20we%20solve%20the%20puzzle>

Bobby, Joel. "Coloring is good for your Health.", Mayo Clinic Health System. (2022) <https://www.mayoclinichealthsystem.org/hometown-health/speaking-of-health/coloring-is-good-for-your-health#:~:text=Coloring%20is%20a%20healthy%20way,feelings%20of%20depression%20and%20anxiety>

Edraki, Mitra et al. "The Effect of Coping Skills Training on Depression, Anxiety, Stress, and Self-Efficacy in Adolescents with Diabetes: A Randomized Controlled Trial." *International journal of community based nursing and midwifery vol. 6,4* (2018): 324–333.

Fey, Alexis. *Managing Anxiety and Mental Health: Coping Strategies for Teens.* Mark Twain Media, Inc., Publishers. (2023)

Logan, Amanda. "Can expressing gratitude improve your mental, physical health?", Mayo Clinic Health System. (2022) <https://www.mayoclinichealthsystem.org/hometown-health/speaking-of-health/can-expressing-gratitude-improve-health#:~:text=Expressing%20gratitude%20is%20associated%20with,everyone%20would%20be%20taking%20it>

Modecki, K.L., Zimmer-Gembeck, M.J. and Guerra, N. "Emotion Regulation, Coping, and Decision Making: Three Linked Skills for Preventing Externalizing Problems in Adolescence." *Child Development, vol. 88,2:* 417–426. (2017) <https://doi.org/10.1111/cdev.12734>

Front Cover Photo Credits:

All front cover photos from istockphoto.com at the file name listed.

Urban Biking- Girl And Boy Riding Bikes In City {© istockphoto.com} gbh007. 17 Dec 2017.
The Artist Draws Anime Comics On Paper. Storyboard For The Cartoon. The Illustrator Creates Sketches For The Book. {© istockphoto.com} Oleksandr Todorov. 26 Sept 2021.
Afro American Woman Writes Down Information In Notebook {© istockphoto.com} brizmaker. 8 Nov 2021.
Teen Guitarist {©istockphoto.com} arieliona. 19 Jun 2010.
Beautiful Young Woman With Long Blonde Hair Meditates In Nature, In A Beautiful Field. Travel And Healthy Lifestyle, Enjoying Nature. {© istockphoto.com} Anna Tretiak. 15 Nov 2022.
Boy Teenager in Checkered Shirt in Red Holds in His Hands Baking Sheet Covered With Parchment With Cookies {© istockphoto.com} Tatsiana Volkava. 3 Dec 2021.
Boy Teen Potter Clay Bowl Working In Pottery Workshop {© istockphoto.com} LUNAMARINA. 22 Sept 2021.